BETTER BY SATURDAY™ SHORT GAME

BETTER
BY
SATURDAY™
SHORT GAME

Featuring Tips by
GOLF MAGAZINE®'s
Top 100 Teachers
with Greg Midland

WARNER BOOKS

NEW YORK   BOSTON

Warner Books

Time Warner Book Group
1271 Avenue of the Americas, New York, NY 10020
Visit our Web site at www.twbookmark.com.

Printed in the United States of America
First Printing: May 2004
10 9 8 7 6 5 4 3 2 1

Library of Congress Cataloging-in-Publication Data
Midland, Greg.
Better by Saturday—short game : featuring tips by Golf magazine's top 100
teachers / Greg Midland.
p. cm.
ISBN 0-446-53259-2
1. Short game (Golf) I. Golf magazine (New York, NY : 1991) II. Title.
GV979.S54M53 2004
796.352'34—dc21   2003010755

Book design by HRoberts Design

CONTENTS

Foreword: Better by *When?*

When I heard the concept of this new series of books, "Better by Saturday," my reaction was immediate: "Hey, it's already Friday." But having seen the series, I'm convinced that the promise of its premise is fulfilled in these pages, which feature some of the best instruction you'll find in a month of Sundays.

If you're like many golf lovers I know, you dream of playing every day, try to play every week, and settle for a bit less than that. An occasional eighteen is better than nothing, but with so much time between rounds, it's tough to groove a swing. How can your muscles remember the inside-out path they took to the ball when you hit that huge drive your last time out? How can you hope to improve, knowing that PGA Tour pros pummel hundreds and even thousands of practice balls for every one you hit?

Here's how. This book contains the best, simplest tips we could get from the game's finest teaching pros, GOLF MAGAZINE's Top 100 Teachers. They work with thousands of ordinary golfers every week, as well as with top amateurs and Tour pros. They are the best in the business. And thanks to our Top 100 Teachers, each of the four books in the Better by Saturday series—they cover driving; iron play and the long game; the short game; and putting—is full of advice that will help you play better your next time out. You don't have to change your swing. Just pay attention. It's easy, since these tips are clear and often entertaining. Even golfers who play every day will learn plenty.

It's all here: everything from teeing a ball up to hitting one off hardpan or out of a tough lie in a fairway bunker. If there's a situation or shot that always ruins your score, you'll find the cure in these pages. If your troubles take a new form every time out, you'll still find ways to shoot a lower score this weekend. And after that, you can re-read this volume for further improvement, or pick up another of our "Better by Saturday" books.

Imagine how good you might get by next month.

Kevin Cook
Editor, GOLF MAGAZINE

Acknowledgments

Many thanks to Mike Malaska and the staff and members of Superstition Golf & Country Club in Superstition Mountain, Arizona, who gave myself and photographer Fred Vuich full access to their two gorgeous Jack Nicklaus–designed courses. Also thanks to both David Huffman and Gary Newkirk for their patience and diligence in helping us to produce the photographs. Finally, thanks to all of GOLF MAGAZINE's Top 100 Teachers, present and past, for the book's most important element: the tips.

—*Greg Midland*

BETTER BY SATURDAY SHORT GAME

Introduction

The short game is golf's version of a trusted relief pitcher in baseball. It can get you out of a tough jam and save the day. Just take it from Tiger Woods, who has said that saving par from a difficult spot near the green is as important to keeping a good round going as sticking an approach shot to two feet and making birdie.

Lest you think that only the best players in the world need a good short game, think again. This quote, from short-game expert Dave Pelz, says it all: "The poorer your game, the more wedges you need." The reason is that while Tour pros hit 13 or 14 greens in regulation per round, the average 10-handicapper hits only four or five. That translates into 13, 14, maybe even 15 wedges, chips, pitches, and bunker shots every time out. So the more greens you miss, the better your short game has to be if you want to score.

How good is your short game? Probably not as sharp as you'd like. Take a cue from the Tour pros; they spend at least 50 percent of their practice time on greenside shots. Even if it's just taking your wedge and hitting some chips in the backyard, the practice will help come Saturday. It might be more fun to bang driver after driver on the range, but that's not going to be the quickest route to becoming a better player.

Other than increasing your practice time, there are several ways to improve your performance around the greens. They involve better techniques, different strategies, and a greater understanding of how the clubs are designed to work to your advantage. This is especially true in a greenside bunker shot, which is a fear-inducing situation for many amateurs.

In this book, GOLF MAGAZINE's Top 100 Teachers take away the fear of short-game miscues. They share their best tips for the shots you see most often around the greens—pitches, chips, and bunker shots—plus a few you don't encounter on a regular basis. Do you know when using a 3-wood from off the green is a wise choice? Or how to tackle a plugged lie in the sand? Those shots, and many more, are explained here.

Armed with this knowledge, you'll have a trusted escape route from almost any greenside shot. And it's a direct route to lower scores.

CHAPTER 1: PITCHING

Stand Tall

Increase your feel on pitch shots with better posture

Standing closer to the ball with a tight, hunched-over stance may seem like it gives you more feel for a pitch shot, but it actually does the opposite. The arms have less room to swing the club back, meaning the backswing gets too far outside and you have to compensate to square the clubface. That's not going to do much for your touch.

When addressing a pitch shot, stand tall, with your back straight and your arms "long." Let your arms hang naturally from your shoulders, creating distance between your hands and legs. The freedom this setup affords allows you to swing the club back smoothly without manipulation, therefore encouraging more feel for the pitch shot at hand. *—**Martin Hall***

QUICK TIP

Practice, Practice, Practice

No matter how long you've played, it's never too late to break the practice-range habit of spending too much time hitting the long ball and too little with the wedges. During a quiet time at your range or local course, hit a variety of pitches from different lies and to different pins, using your pitching, sand, and lob wedges. This valuable short-game practice will translate to strokes saved during your rounds. *—Shelby Futch*

The Low Runner

When the situation allows, keep your pitch trajectory low

The easiest shot to hit close, especially if you have limited practice time, is a pitch that runs most of the way to the hole instead of one that flies in the air. You can save strokes by recognizing when, and how, to play the low-trajectory pitch.

You'll need a green that is open in front, relatively flat, and has plenty of room between your ball and the hole. Using a pitching wedge, position the ball just inside the right heel. Set most of your weight over your left foot, which encourages a clean, descending blow. Swing the club back fairly low, and lead it through with the left hand. This will de-loft the clubface and set up a low follow-through that gets the ball running quickly.

—*Fred Griffin*

Lob It

Two simple keys to hit the lob shot high and close

Learn to play the lob shot well, and you'll have a recovery tool when you need to pitch the ball high and soft to a tight pin. Keep in mind that the first requirement for a lob is a good lie with the ball sitting on top of the grass.

To preserve maximum loft through impact, use a weak left-hand position on the club. Rotate your left hand toward the target, then re-grip the club. The "V" between your left thumb and forefinger should now point just inside your right shoulder. For the swing, your thought should be "shaft back up, shaft back through." You will have to use plenty of wrist cock to get the shaft nearly vertical on both ends. —**Dick Harmon**

QUICK TIP

Hold the Finish

Feedback is the secret of golf, and it's as important in the short game as it is in the full swing. You must pay attention to how your finesse shots feel, so you can evaluate what you did right and what needs improvement. Do this by holding your finish after hitting a shot, staying in position until you see the ball hit the ground. This is especially important in practice, but holding your finish on the course can give you an indicator to how sharp your short game really is. —*Dave Pelz*

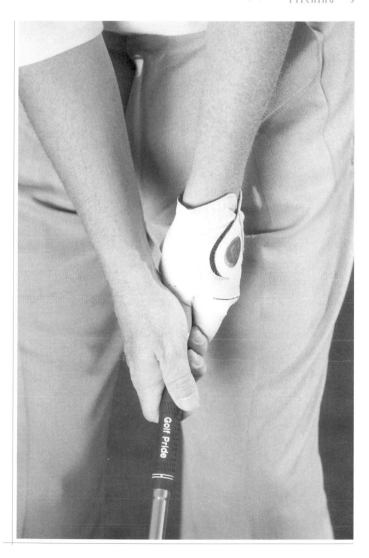

Parachute to Safety

How to float the ball over a bunker without fail

The anxiety of the sand makes pitching over a bunker a tougher shot than it really is. Stick to the basics: Don't try to hit the shot pro-style and cut across the ball from out to in. You can fly the ball high and drop it softly—as if it were hanging from a parachute—without doing anything fancy.

Position the ball inside your left heel with your stance slightly open and the clubface aimed at the flag [photo 1]. Grip the club lightly to keep your wrists soft and allow them to hinge freely on the backswing [photo 2]. Here's the key: To keep your head behind the ball for maximum loft, feel like you're peeking under the ball as you approach impact. Accelerate the club to a high finish. —***Phil Ritson***

Center the Shaft

Set the club in the right place to take advantage of the loft

Your trusted club for higher pitch shots is the sand wedge. While the club has plenty of loft to begin with, you want to preserve it through the pitch swing in order to hit the ball as high as possible. The way to do this is in the setup.

In order to maximize the club's loft, set up with the shaft pointing at the center of your body, toward the belt buckle. The shaft should be straight up and down, with your hands even with or slightly behind the ball. Resist the temptation to angle the shaft forward; this de-lofts the club and produces a lower shot.

—Mike Adams

Keep Moving

Look to your legs to initiate the pitch shot downswing

Poor results on pitch shots often come from the lower body freezing on the downswing. When the hands and arms are doing all the work, the swing becomes less smooth and the wrists often flip the club through impact—not a good way to hit the ball solid.

To make sure the lower body has its proper role in the pitch swing, start your downswing by rolling your right ankle and knee toward the target. This move helps get your weight shifting to your left side and keeps everything—hands, arms, club, and body—in sync. The club will come into the ball from the correct angle of approach for crisp contact every time. **—Paul Trittler**

Unlock Your Chest

Rotate your upper body in rhythm with the club for solid pitches

"Keep your weight forward" is good advice for the pitch shot. It becomes troublesome when you translate it to "don't move." Good pitchers of the ball allow their upper body to move with their arm swing, producing a rhythmic motion that leads to the best contact [photo 1].

Your body has to keep pace with the movement of the wrists through impact, which gives the shot its height and spin. If you're trying to keep your head down—there's that "don't move" thought again—the temptation is to stop your body and hit at the ball, which leads to poor contact. Instead, turn your upper body in rhythm with the swinging clubhead, and face the target after impact [photo 2]. —*T. J. Tomasi*

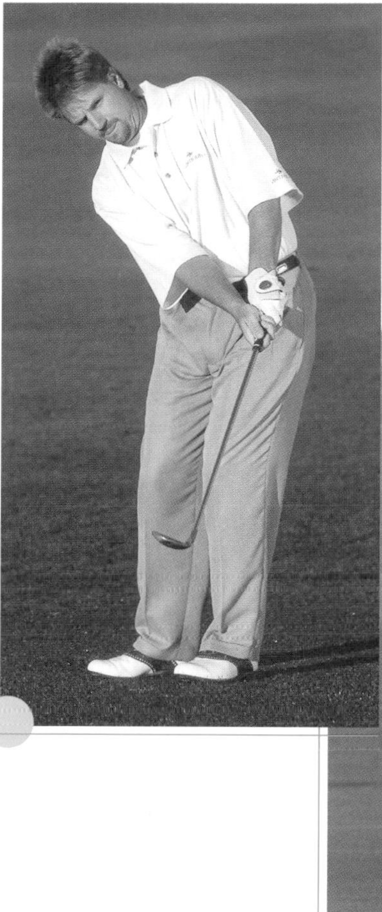

1

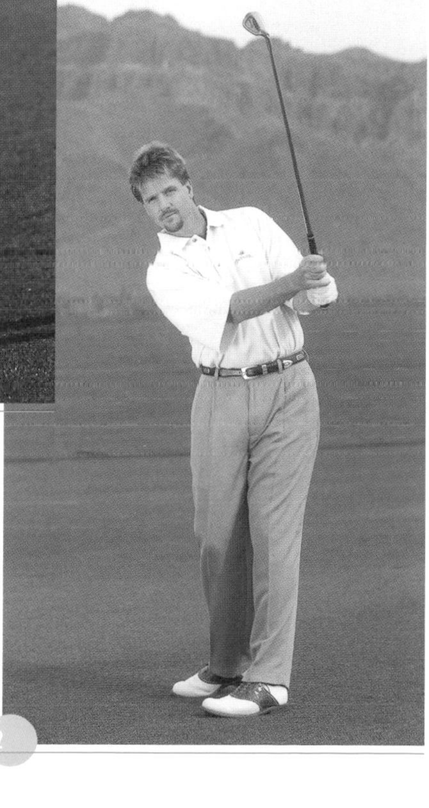

2

Long and Low

You can consistently hit the ball high by keeping the club low

Ask most golfers to hit a short, high pitch, and they flip the club upward through impact. This is one way to add loft, but it's tough to make this move without hitting chunks and skulls. The fact is, you rarely need more loft than a squarely hit sand wedge provides.

To better execute the short, high pitch, focus on swinging the clubhead "long and low along the line" after impact [photo 1]. If the clubhead hugs the ground, the leading edge slides under the ball and pops it out of the grass. Trust the club's loft, and think of it as a shallow sweep through the ball. You'll make more consistent contact and still get plenty of height [photo 2].

—Craig Shankland

Underhand Toss

A drill to help you feel the proper pace of a pitch swing

Two factors control a pitch shot's distance: the swing's length, and the swing's pace. A shorter pitch demands a shorter swing at a slower pace; a longer pitch demands a longer swing at a faster pace.

The variations in swing length and pace are sometimes tough to feel from just practicing shots. Try this drill: Hold a sand wedge in your left hand and a ball in your right hand. Practice swinging back and through, tossing the ball underhanded to targets of different distances. The longer the toss, the faster and longer the arm swing should be. Translate this feeling into your pitch shots to gain a better feel for controlling distance.

—Mike McGetrick

QUICK TIP

Rhythm Method

Good rhythm is crucial to successful pitching. But it's difficult to swing rhythmically if the lengths of the backswing and follow-through don't match. A short backswing causes over-acceleration at impact; a long backswing leads to deceleration. Strive to make your back- and throughswings equal in length. Once you do, you'll have better distance control and improve your pitching success. **—Keith Lyford**

Handle Adjustment

Lower the end of the club at address to hit the ball higher

The next time you face a pitch that you have to get in the air quickly, imagine trying to hit the shot softly using a 7-iron. You'd have to make some adjustments, namely opening the clubface and lowering the handle of the club toward the ground in order to make a steeper swing.

Apply these same adjustments when hitting the shot with a sand or lob wedge. The higher you want the ball to fly, the lower you should set the club's handle at address, with your hands behind the ball to set the clubface open. This forces you to stand farther from the ball and widen your stance, which helps maintain your knee flex and lob the ball high and soft.

—Mike Lopuszynski

Rough Pitch

Favor your front side to pitch the ball cleanly out of the rough

Always use a lob or sand wedge when hitting a medium to high pitch from the rough. The lie needs to dictate how you play the shot; if it's poor, be satisfied with simply getting the ball safely onto the green. But even if it's only moderately heavy grass, a small setup adjustment will help you hit the shot crisply.

The club's angle of approach needs to be steeper from the rough. To achieve this, position your head slightly in front of the ball, with your weight favoring your front leg. Open the clubface, and then take your grip, hovering the club slightly at address rather than resting it on the ground. This setup encourages a downward blow; keep the clubface pointing at the sky after impact to send the ball high. *—Jim Flick*

CHAPTER 2: CHIPPING

Rough Stab

When you can't chip it, chop it out of heavy rough

For a chip from thick, gnarly rough just off the green, you need to control the club through the grass and hit the ball with touch. Played with a conventional chipping stroke, the grass would grab the club and slow its momentum, making distance control nearly impossible.

Play the stab shot instead. Using a sand wedge, position the ball a couple inches behind your right foot, and align the clubface square to the target. On the backswing, cock your wrists as if you were hammering a nail, and hit down nearly on top of the ball with virtually no follow-through. The ball will pop out low and run straight ahead, making distance more predictable. **—Don Trahan**

QUICK TIP

Club Selection

After determining the lie of the chip and slope of the green, your club selection process isn't quite through. Once your choice is in your hands, test it out by waggling the club while staring at the line you've selected to play the shot. You want to both see and feel the shot with the club in your hands; if you can't, choose a different club. *—Rina Ritson*

Left-Side Drill

Train the left hand to stay square for crisper chips

Chipping mis-hits often occur when the wrists flip the clubhead forward on the downswing, causing fat or thin contact. Impact should be a descending blow, with the hands leading the clubhead into the ball. The key is to keep the left hand square through the motion. To help feel this, grip the club with your left hand only, and grip your left forearm with your right hand. This prevents the back of the left hand from twisting on the backswing, which often leads to the wrists flipping at impact. Play the ball off your right toe, and hit a few chips this way until you feel how the left hand remains stable and leads the motion. When you grip the club normally, re-create this feeling for crisp contact. **—*Rick Smith***

QUICK TIP

Look Ahead

When addressing a chip, focus on a spot in front of the ball. This promotes leaning slightly toward the target at address. From this position, the swing will be more upright, creating a sharp, descending blow and crisp contact. **—*Laird Small***

Perfect Setup

Ball position and shaft angle are two keys you can preset at address

You can't chip it close if you start from a poor setup. Two of the most common errors that lead to inconsistent contact are faulty ball position (too far forward) and a shaft angle that leans back instead of forward. Here are two keys to remember every time. Play the ball off your back foot to ensure a slightly descending approach to impact, so the club strikes the ball before it strikes the ground. Next, angle the shaft toward the target so your hands are forward and the club's grip end is even with your left thigh. This de-lofts the clubface to maximize roll and helps keep the wrists firm throughout the stroke. The ball will fly fairly low and roll most of the way to the hole. —*John Gerring*

A Little Wrist Action

Use a little wrist action and lower-body movement for chipping

Ignore the old advice to "chip like you putt." When all wrist and leg motion is restricted, the result is a stiff motion that decreases feel and usually results in weak chips that come up short of the hole.

To free up your chipping stroke and nip the ball cleanly, set up by bending more at the waist and putting more weight over the left foot. Let your right wrist hinge slightly on the backswing to release tension and enhance your feel for distance. On the forward swing, let your knees shift toward the target while the hands lead the clubhead into the ball. Working your lower body and wrists together will add rhythm to your chipping and allow you to hit the ball the correct distance. **—*Jim Suttie***

Solid Long Chips

The lower body should lead the way on long chips

When you're chipping from at least 10 yards off the green, or you're going for a back pin, the legs need to figure into the motion. Otherwise you'll come up short. Freezing the lower body on these longer chips results in inconsistent contact and an unnatural, mechanical stroke.

Let your lower body react naturally to the swinging of the arms and upper body. Try starting the downswing by shifting the knees toward the target, which transfers your weight forward and gives your chipping motion some added momentum. Don't scoop at the ball with the right hand to try adding distance. Just let the knees lead and you'll pinch the ball off the grass.

—Rick Grayson

Shaft Angle

Use a tee to make sure you're using the club correctly on chips

The shaft angle you set at address (leaning toward the target) is crucial in chipping. But it's not enough just to have it at the beginning; you should strive to maintain this shaft angle through the motion. This improves your chances for crisp contact.

To check that you're not losing this shaft angle during the chip, stick a tee in the end of the grip so it points to your left hip at address. Chip a ball to a hole and hold your finish—the tee should be pointing outside the left side of your body, toward your chest. If it points back toward your hips, you've lost the shaft angle and tried to scoop the ball. Adding a little forward body turn to your downswing will help keep the hands quiet and improve your results. **—Gary Wiren**

Chipping Grip

Adjust the way you hold the club to hit better chips

Instead of chipping with a normal grip—with the palms facing each other—turn the back of your left hand down so the knuckles face down to the ground at address. Hold the club in the palm of your left hand, with the handle along your lifeline. This will lock the back of your left hand in the "down" position.

Now strengthen your right-hand grip, turning it to the right, so the knuckles are underneath the shaft [photo 1]. This alternate grip will help you deliver the club to the ball with the hands ahead. Think about a follow-through in which your left elbow and the logo on your glove move forward through impact [photo 2], a move that is easier to make with this special chipping grip.

—Bill Harmon

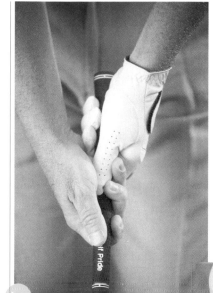

Stay Left

Use the "right heel up" drill to keep your weight forward

A common chipping fault is leaning away from the target at address, which makes your weight drift to your right (rear) foot during the chip. Your weight then tends to stay back through impact, causing chunks and chili-dips.

Here's a drill to help keep your weight on your front foot from the start. Take your normal chipping address, then raise your right heel a few inches off the ground, keeping the toe planted. Now practice hitting chips in this position, feeling how your weight never drifts away from the target. Always try to keep this "anchored" feeling when you chip; you'll trap the ball against the ground for better contact. **—Gary Smith**

Stiff Arm

Hit better chips by keeping the right arm "long"

Consistency in chipping can be boiled down to one element: the club's angle of attack. For best contact, the club must be on its downward arc when it meets the ball. Key on your right arm to get this downward angle every time.

A faulty arc is preset at address, specifically bending your right arm and lowering your right shoulder, as if to hit a tee shot. Instead, focus on keeping your right arm "long," or fully extended, at address. This results in the shoulders being fairly level. Now at impact, straighten your right arm again, creating a steeper angle of attack and solid contact. **—*Mitchell Spearman***

QUICK TIP

Lie Adjustments

When the ball is in a bare lie or sitting down in rough, you need a more descending blow to ensure crisp contact. Move the ball back outside the right toe and choose a club with more loft—e.g., a 9-iron instead of a 7-iron. Moving the ball back reduces the effective loft on the club, so the shot tends to fly lower and roll farther. *—Jeff Warne*

Look Away

Focus on the target to groove a smooth chipping stroke

Good chippers make a smooth, rhythmic motion, letting the ball get in the way of the clubhead. Poor chippers focus so much on hitting the ball that they flinch as they approach impact. This sudden movement of the hands and wrists, which causes thin or fat contact, is another version of the "yips."

To avoid the chipping yips, try hitting chip shots while looking at the target instead of the ball. Try this first in practice, and then in play. Since the swing is so short, you won't have trouble hitting the ball, and looking at the target will take the flinch out of your motion. You'll make a smoother stroke and hit the chip the right distance. *—**Steve Bosdosh***

Chest to Ball

Hit your chips better by matching your sternum to your ball position

Your sternum is your swing center in chipping. When setting up with the ball back and your weight forward, the two are not in the same place, meaning the club will not bottom out at the ball for solid contact. The goal is for your ball position and your sternum to line up. Do that, and you'll see your chipping improve.

Here's an easy way to make sure your sternum is in line with the ball. Take your address, with your weight favoring the front foot, then raise the club and extend it out from your chest perpendicular to the target line. From there, adjust your ball position so it's under the shaft. Now you're lined up and ready to go.

—*Jane Frost*

CHAPTER 3: SAND PLAY

Sure Out

Strengthen your right hand to escape the sand with a shallow swing

A weak grip in the sand accounts for weak results. Placing the right hand too much on top of the shaft—so that the "V" of your thumb and forefinger points at your chin—encourages a swing that is too steep and takes too much sand.

A shallower swing arc is best for greenside bunker play. To promote a shallower swing, strengthen the right hand on the grip of the club at address. The "V" should point toward your right shoulder. This helps you bring the club back a little flatter, so the club comes down into the sand on a shallower angle and skims through easily. The ball will be lifted out softly onto the green.

—*Dick Farley*

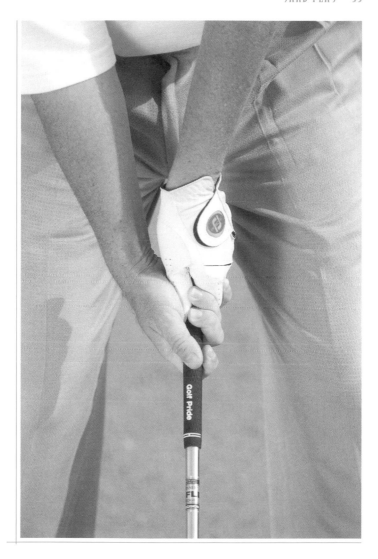

Stop Scooping

Get on your toes to learn how to blast the ball out

Instead of hanging back on your right side and trying to scoop the ball out of the sand, the hips need to rotate to allow the body to turn toward the target at impact. Turning the hips helps you swing the club into the sand with a slight downward blow, so the ball gets carried out on a cushion of sand without you helping it out.

To ingrain this turning of the hips, hit practice sand shots with your right foot pulled back and on its toes. This forces the hips to turn to the target on the downswing, so you're rotating over your left leg rather than falling back on the right leg. You'll blast the ball out of the sand every time. —***Todd Sones**

QUICK TIP

The Only Must
The only true fundamental for greenside bunker shots is getting the center of gravity of the clubface under the center of the ball. Do this, and the sand you displace will force the ball upward with enough loft for most situations. For a basic, get-on-the-green bunker shot, swinging the clubhead under the ball should be your primary thought. —*Rick Whitfield*

Step Through

To hit a severe downhill bunker shot, you have to let your body go

When your ball is perched on a severe downhill slope in a bunker, you can counteract the lie by setting 90 percent of your weight on your front foot at address, and aligning your shoulders parallel to the slope. But if the slope is steep enough that your body wants to step through after impact, that's exactly what you should do.

It is very hard to keep your balance—and not fall on your face—when the forward momentum of the swing [photo 1] takes you down the slope. Immediately after impact, step through with your back foot as you look to see where the ball is flying [photo 2]. Walking through the shot, though unusual, will let your body and club move forward naturally, helping you make a better swing. **—Dave Pelz**

Address Angle

After taking the proper grip, lay the shaft of the club back

Opening the clubface to address a greenside bunker shot is good advice. Just make sure you do it right. First rotate the clubface open about 10 degrees, then place both hands on the club. If you take your grip first and then rotate the club open, it will return to square during the swing and you'll lose the benefit of added loft.

After taking your proper grip, lay the club shaft away from the target as you address the ball. By creating a small angle between the shaft and your left arm, the sole will more easily slide through the sand and carry the ball out high and soft.

—Bill Harmon

QUICK TIP

Fly the Sand

Pick a spot on the green where you want the ball to land, then concentrate on swinging through so the sand flies to that spot. This will help you achieve your primary objective, which is to get the ball out of trouble and onto the green. For all shots, start with a slightly open stance and splash the sand to the spot you picked out. *—Peter Krause*

Shallow Escape

Flatten out your swing when faced with a short, uphill bunker shot

A short, uphill bunker shot of 10 or 15 yards demands a precise hit, not a steep blast that explodes a big scoop of sand into the air. This often causes the club to dig into the sand, lose momentum, and leave the ball in the bunker.

Try swinging more slowly and on a much flatter plane to hit a fast-climbing, soft shot. Take a moderately open stance with the ball opposite your left (front) heel. Set your hands slightly behind the ball at address, and then make a flat, arms-controlled backswing. Aim for a spot about an inch behind the ball, and don't worry about a full follow-through, because the club is going to swing into the slope. The ball will pop out over the lip and toward the hole. **—David Glenz**

Divot Drill

Stay "in the box" to make the ideal bunker divot

Typically, bunker mis-hits come from hitting too far behind the ball, meaning the clubhead enters and leaves the sand too early in the swing. Devote some practice time to improving your sand divot, and better bunker play will follow.

Draw an 8- to 10-inch box in the sand and divide it into thirds. Place a ball on the line closest to the back edge, and focus your eyes on the back line. After making your swing, look down to make sure the divot hole starts at the back line and runs to the front line. This indicates the club slid underneath the ball properly and lifted it out softly. Envision this box on every bunker shot for better results. **—Phil Rodgers**

Follow Through

Use the over-the-shoulder drill to help ingrain a good finish

Few things in golf are worse than having to hit the same shot over again. This happens all too often in greenside bunker shots: The fear of catching the ball thin causes you to hit it heavy, and the ball stays in the bunker. Focus on the finish to stop hitting it fat.

The ball won't leave the bunker if you don't follow through. To encourage a full finish, scoop a large mound of sand onto your clubface, take your address, and swing forward to the finish. Feel like you're throwing the sand over your left shoulder [photos 1, 2, and 3]. Now concentrate on reaching that position in your actual swing, finishing with your weight forward and the club over your shoulder. You'll make better contact and avoid the fat bunker shot. —*Mike Bender*

Smoother When Wet

Learn to make adjustments when hitting from wet, packed sand

The texture of sand can vary from bunker to bunker—and so should your technique. One of the toughest situations for amateurs to handle is when the ball is sitting in firm, wet sand, which makes it easy to hit the shot thin.

First, consider using a pitching wedge, which has a sharper leading edge that's better suited to digging into the cement-like surface. Close the clubface slightly at address to help the club penetrate the sand and slide under the ball. Make a longer than normal backswing, and swing into the ball with a controlled downswing and an abbreviated follow-through. The clubhead should dig quickly into the sand and pop the ball out with some backspin. —*Dan Pasquariello*

QUICK TIP

Leave the Ball

You don't want to plow sand into the ball to propel it forward, you want to slide the clubface underneath it. The physics are similar to the trick of pulling a table-cloth out from under a table full of dishes: You want to "leave the ball" in the sand by making a fast, sliding motion with the club, as if you're cutting the legs out from under the ball. —*Craig Shankland*

Uphill Slopes

Angle yourself for success when the ball is above your feet

Uneven lies in the bunker are a challenge, but the good news is that all of the changes are in your setup, not your swing. In the case of the ball above your feet, it involves angling your body to manage the effects of the slope.

First, open your stance. This allows you to turn through the shot easily and sets your weight into the slope for better balance. Angle your shoulders to match the slope, and position your hands so the shaft of the club is perpendicular to the hill and pointing right at the ball. These adjustments help the club bottom out in the right place, rather than taking too much or too little sand. You can make your normal swing and escape as if hitting from a flat lie. **—Mike Adams**

The Short of It

Hit the short bunker shot with touch and control

For an extremely short bunker shot, it's common to control distance by hitting farther behind the ball. This can create inconsistent results. Simply vary your setup and technique slightly to become a master of this delicate situation.

Use a lob wedge for maximum loft, and open the clubface generously at address. Then grip down, almost to the metal of the shaft, which encourages a short but aggressive swing [photo 1]. Keep your weight left, pick the club up abruptly with your wrist cock on the backswing, and then kick your right knee toward the target on the downswing. This will help you avoid trying to scoop the ball onto the green. The follow-through will be short as your hips and arms rotate to the left after impact [photo 2]. —*Fred Griffin*

Wing It

Let your left arm play chicken for greenside bunker shots

To hit a high, soft shot from a greenside bunker, you need to hold the clubface open while your body rotates through impact. This allows the sand wedge's bounce to slide through the sand, lofting the ball out. Help hold the face open by making a move that you want to avoid in the full swing: Fold the left arm into a "chicken wing" on the follow-through. First, open your stance and clubface at address. Then on the downswing, keep your arms relaxed and your chest rotating toward the target as you swing the club along your stance line from out to in. This creates the chicken wing and keeps the clubface pointing at the sky after impact. **—Patti McGowan**

CHAPTER 4: STRATEGY

Avoid Fat Pitches

Keys that will help you avoid chunking your greenside pitches

There are few outcomes more frustrating than hitting a pitch shot heavy, especially if it falls into a bunker or other hazard. The next time your ball is sitting in greenside rough, take a few steps to avoid hitting the shot fat. Begin by making some practice swings to identify where the club contacts the grass, then play the ball one inch farther back from that point. This ball position, in addition to setting about 60 percent of your weight to the left at address, ensures that the club will contact the ball before the ground. Allow gravity to regulate the speed of your downswing to maintain a good rhythm. The clubhead should feel as if it's falling on its own toward the ball, then brushing the grass at impact. *—Laird Small*

QUICK TIP

Smart Practice

Redirect focus and practice time to your short game. Work on getting your bunker shots to the hole, hitting your pitches the correct distances, and so on. Even if you don't hit the ball with tremendous power, spending more of your practice time on the short game allows you to compete with longer players. *—Lynn Marriott*

Hover the Club

Make crisp contact on chips by suspending the club above the grass

Especially if your poor contact around the greens tends to be fat, your problem may stem from soling the clubhead deep into the grass. This puts the club's leading edge below the ball. Since the swing will tend to bottom out wherever you set the club down, soling it deep leads to heavy contact. You've probably seen Tour players hover the clubhead of their driver when addressing a ball on a tee. Applied to your short greenside shots, this concept will encourage you to swing downward into the ball. Hover the clubhead at the ball's equator, feeling its weight as you prepare to take it back. Your swing will bottom out right at the ball, leading to better contact. **—Jim Flick**

Tough Spot #1

Play the percentages when your ball finds rough over the green

When you air-mail the green with your approach shot, the temptation is to play a delicate shot that lands on the fringe and trickles to the hole. The odds are against you: Because the pin is cut close to the back of the green, you'll have to land the ball on a dime— come up short and you'll again be playing from the rough.

Play the percentages: Take a 7- or 8-iron and chip the ball into the bank [photo 1], letting it bounce a few times before reaching the putting surface [photo 2]. A ball hit along the ground is much easier to control than one hit high in the air, and the chances of leaving it short are slim. While you may not stiff it close, you'll have a makable putt and reduce your chances of wasting strokes. **—*Craig Bunker***

Tough Spot #2

Take the safe route when your ball rests on the edge of a bunker

This situation doesn't happen often, which makes it all the more frustrating. When the ball rests on the lip of the bunker, half in sand and half in grass, the lie makes contact unpredictable. Adjust your strategy accordingly.

Don't even look at the hole, especially if you'd have to loft the ball over the bunker to get there. Aim to the fat part of the green, and play this shot like a chip: Take your pitching wedge, keeping the swing short and simple. Set most of your weight left to ensure that the club makes contact with the ball before the ground. It's your best chance for escaping and avoiding a big number. **—*Craig Bunker***

Assess the Shot

Craft a plan for greenside shots based on the lie and situation

One mistake that leads to lost strokes around the greens is going ahead with a shot without assessing it properly. Your first step should be to inspect the lie by running your hand around the ball, touching the blades of grass only. This gives you an idea of how far down the clubhead must go to make solid contact with the ball.

Once you've made your club selection, make a "five-second stare down." Stand near the ball and really look at the shot. Think about how far you want to carry the ball, and most importantly, what you must do to hole it. Don't entertain any negative thoughts; be positive and you'll have success. **—*Craig Harmon***

QUICK TIP

Too Much Finesse

If you tend to "get cute" with your short game and try a riskier shot than is needed, it's time to cut down on the fancy stuff. Remember that golf is a game of numbers—low score wins. Resign yourself to a more conservative approach around the greens, selecting the high-percentage play even if it leaves you with 12- or 15-foot putts. *—Dr. Richard Coop*

Flare Stance

Open your stance the right way for best results on short shots

You've likely heard that you should address short greenside shots with an open stance, which is good advice. Keeping your stance square acts like a wall: It stops the body from swinging, killing the acceleration and free-flowing motion that are necessary for a good short game.

Just make sure you achieve an open stance the correct way. If your first move is to open either the upper or lower body, or pull the front foot away from the target line, you're setting yourself up for inconsistent contact.

Instead, start with both feet perpendicular to the target line. Then, keeping your heel planted, flare your left toe open 30 to 40 degrees. This position keeps your hips and shoulders square, while encouraging a smooth swing that will extend into a high, full finish. **—Dave Pelz**

Stroll to the Hole

A preswing key to help you chip it close

Your score would likely improve greatly if you got more of your chip shots up and down. But often because golfers feel rushed, they don't take the time to properly gauge the chip at hand. Without that knowledge, it's difficult to chip the ball close.

The next time you play, walk from your ball to the hole and get a feel for the entire shot. Pace off the distance and start to develop a shot plan, paying particular attention to the green's slope. This will affect your club selection and where you will aim the clubface. Walking back, pause near the spot where you want the ball to land and make a rehearsal swing. This helps provide a mental picture of the shot so you can chip it near the hole.

—Lynn Marriott

Take the 8-Iron

When faced with a long bunker shot, leave the sand wedge in the bag

A long greenside bunker shot—50 to 75 yards—deserves plenty of respect, but it doesn't have to be feared. Keep in mind, however, that it becomes nearly impossible to pull off if you try to blast the ball out with your sand wedge.

For more consistency, use your 8-iron. The key is to open the clubface so the club's sole will have some bounce when it hits the sand. This prevents the club from digging too deep. Set up as you would for a short greenside shot, with your stance and body aligned open. Use a controlled, three-quarter swing and hit the sand about an inch behind the ball. It will fly on a lower trajectory and roll forward a little after landing. **—*Martin Hall***

CHAPTER 5: SPECIALTY SHOTS

Plugged Up

Get the ball out of a plugged lie in the sand

It can be disheartening to arrive at a bunker and see your ball plugged on the upslope. Relax. It's true the shot isn't easy, but it doesn't have to be that hard. In fact, the technique for blasting it out can be pretty reliable. As with any uphill lie, you'll have a problem getting the ball to the hole because the slope increases the effective loft of the club. To counteract this effect, take one more stick than usual, using a pitching wedge instead of a sand wedge. Position the ball forward in your stance, with your hands slightly ahead and your shoulders parallel to the slope. Swing through the sand with plenty of force, striving for a full finish.

—*Dave Pelz*

QUICK TIP

A Secure Grip

Short-game shots require sensitivity, meaning your hands need to be allowed to feel the weight of the clubhead. Be aware of the minimum amount of tension needed for solid contact. Think "fingers secure, arms relaxed" when you grip the club. This gives you a trusted hold on the club while giving your arms the freedom to respond to the swinging of the clubhead. *—Jim Flick*

Trap the Ball

Make your setup mirror impact on half-wedge shots

The half-wedge, from about 50 to 60 yards out, is one of golf's most dreaded shots. The key is not to try to help the ball in the air; the club's descending angle of approach will give you all the loft you need. Set up to the ball with a position that encourages you to trap the ball at impact. Position the ball just behind the middle of your stance, then angle the shaft of the club toward the target so the hands are ahead of the ball. This promotes a downward, trapping action at impact. Focus your eyes on the front side of the ball with your weight favoring your left, and you'll make solid contact to hit the ball the right distance. **—Kent Cayce**

On the Collar

Play the bellied wedge when a standard chip won't do

There are plenty of tricky spots where your ball can end up around the green. One such place is on the collar, up against the rough. The grass sticking up behind the ball prevents you from playing a standard chip, or using a putter.

Keep it simple from the collar, and give yourself a chance to save par, by playing the bellied wedge. Use a pitching wedge and position the ball off the inside of your right heel. Hold the club slightly off the ground so the leading edge is at the ball's equator. Make an arms-and-shoulders pendulum stroke, holding the wrists firm. Stroke the club a little longer than you would for a putt from this distance; the ball will come off with overspin and roll to the hole. **—Dick Tiddy**

When Backward Is Better

Turn your back to the target and escape from this difficult spot

Your ball sits outside the high lip of a bunker, meaning you're going to have to stand in the bunker with the ball well above your feet. Even if you are able to make solid contact, which is doubtful, the natural loft of a wedge will pull the ball well left of the target.

Believe it or not, a better way to hit this shot is backward. Stand very close to the ball so your swing is almost vertical. Position the ball just ahead of your toe line, put your left hand on your right shoulder, and hinge the club away from the target with your right hand only. A bigger backswing is necessary because you won't generate much wrist action through impact. Keeping your right shoulder in place, chop down on the ball and finish your follow-through. **—*Dave Pelz***

Limit Your Backswing

Control is your goal when playing a partial wedge shot

Whenever you're making a less than full swing, control of the club becomes critical. Trying to reduce power by freezing the body and making a steep, hands-and-arms motion promotes a downswing that is too quick. This burst of speed makes contact and distance unpredictable.

Think about the length of the shot at hand, and how that translates to the backswing. For instance, a 50-yard wedge shot requires about half of your normal backswing. Figure your left arm should reach the 9 o'clock position. Let your wrists cock slightly, with the arms under more control and the shaft well short of vertical. Once you get the feel for control, you'll find the distances of your partial wedge shots to be more reliable. *—Carl Welty*

High Spin

When and how to put "juice" on your wedge shots

Putting maximum spin on a wedge shot, useful when playing to a tight pin position, requires the right lie. Specifically, the ball must be lying cleanly, with little or no grass behind it. If that's the case, you can ensure some spin on the ball by working on the right club position after impact.

For increased backspin, the right arm should not rotate over the left as the club passes impact. Take some practice swings, and work on rotating the entire right side through the shot to promote good acceleration and prevent "scooping," where the clubhead passes the hands before impact. You want to feel as if the ball is pinched against the clubface, trapped between the grooves and the ground. *—**Bill Moretti***

Wood Chip

Sometimes a fairway wood can come in handy around the greens

You've seen the Tour pros chip from off the green with a fairway wood, and it can be a valuable arsenal in *your* game as well. Use it when the ball is sitting up in light greenside rough very close to the putting surface and the hole—a situation where playing a regular chip shot might give you less distance control and lead to a mis-hit.

Take your 3-wood and grip down almost to the shaft, with the ball forward of center. Push your hands slightly ahead of the ball and make a smooth, level motion, like an elongated putting stroke. The ball will jump off the top of the grass and roll onto the putting surface. With a little practice, you'll find that the wide clubface makes solid contact a breeze. **—Gary Smith**

St. Andrews Runner

Minimum air time, maximum ground time is the key to this shot

Use a 4-iron for this shot made popular in Scotland. The requirements are that the ball must be lying in short fairway grass, with a tremendous amount of green between it and the hole. Often, this shot is played to a pin on a top tier, when flying it to the hole is not practical.

The longer shaft creates more leverage, so you don't have to make a very long swing at all. Play the ball in the middle of your stance, and hold the club firmly with the last three fingers of your left hand. This helps keep the hands ahead of the clubhead through impact [see photo 1]. Allow your knees to shift forward a bit on the downswing; the ball will come off very low and behave like a putt, rolling most of the way to the hole [photo 2]. **—Martin Hall**

Uphill Chip

A few setup adjustments will help you on an upslope

The key when chipping the ball from an uphill slope is to stick with your regular chipping motion, but make some setup adjustments to counterbalance the hill. Just remember this: Your weight and ball position shift in the same direction—in this case toward the target.

Play the ball just forward of center in your stance, and set your weight favoring your left side. This will anchor your body into the hill for stability. Take one more club, as the uphill lie will add loft to the shot. It will also tend to throw the shot left, so open the clubface slightly and try to keep it open after impact. Keep your weight steady on your left side through the stroke, and the ball will fly to the target. **—Bill Moretti**.

QUICK TIP

Lob Laws

Don't fall into the trap of using the lob wedge when another club is better suited to hitting the high-percentage shot. Here are some situations when the lob wedge should stay in your bag: anything from an uphill lie, long bunker shots, and pitches into the wind. In these cases, the added loft of a lob wedge will only make it harder to get up and down. *—Dave Pelz*

For more golf tips, as well as news, travel advice, equipment updates, and more, visit **GOLF MAGAZINE** on the web at www.golfonline.com.